C000270091

The Creed

BELIEF IN ACTION

CWR

Phin Hall

Contents

Introduction

'I do believe; help me overcome my unbelief!'
(Mark 9:24)

Many years ago I was a choirboy in my local village church. Having no real experience of church, I was surprised to discover that the services were not quite as I had expected. Far from consisting of pious onlookers sitting in rapt attention as we sang beautiful hymns with our angelic voices, most of the time was spent reciting various incomprehensible phrases. Included in these recitations were two creeds, both of which have been etched into my memory ever since. The creeds in question were the Apostles' Creed and the Nicene Creed. Neither their names nor their content meant anything to me at the time, and I often wondered why we kept reciting them. Even when I began to understand the significance of the creeds, I couldn't see the point in constantly reminding ourselves of what we believe.

The origins of these creeds are found back in Jesus' departing words to His disciples in Matthew 28:19: 'Therefore go and make disciples of all nations, baptising them in the name of the Father and of the Son and of the Holy Spirit.' It is believed that, in response to this command, the Church developed the practice of asking baptismal candidates to profess their faith, as follows: 'I believe in God the Father. I believe in Jesus Christ, the Son of God. I believe in the Holy Spirit.' Thus the creed was born. All the additional phrases in the later creeds, which were usually added to defend the Church against various heresies as they arose, were simply developments of these three basic statements of faith.

During the first few hundred years of its life the Church suffered varying degrees of persecution and groups of local Christians throughout the Roman empire ended up cut off from each other, sometimes for many years. As a result, a number of different creeds emerged, such as the Creed of Antioch, the Old Roman Creed, the Creed of Jerusalem and the Creed of Alexandria, all of which built upon that original formula of belief in God the Father, Jesus and the Holy Spirit. The best known of these early creeds is the Apostles' Creed.

It has been said that it got its name because the twelve Apostles gathered together and, one by one, they each delivered a statement, the creed being the end result. It's a good story, but unfortunately it's also nonsense. The true history of the Apostles' Creed is shrouded in mystery, but it is believed to have been set in its present form at some point in the second century.

This and most other creeds tend to follow a set pattern, based on those early baptismal statements:
• I believe in God, followed by such descriptions as 'Father' and 'Creator'
• I believe in Jesus, followed by statements about His death and resurrection
• I believe in the Holy Spirit
• I believe in the Church
• I believe in salvation and eternal life.

The formerly scattered bishops came together shortly after the Church's rise to favour in Rome in order to settle on a single creed for use throughout the Church. Taking this same pattern, they produced, over a number of years, what is known as the Nicene Creed. These two creeds have been used as a statement of faith throughout the Church ever since, and while this study guide will focus on the Apostles' Creed (referred to throughout as 'the Creed'), we will also consider some of the additions of the Nicene Creed because they will help us to get a firmer grasp on what it truly important – those beliefs that set us apart as Christians.

That said, the question of why we should keep reminding ourselves of what we believe still remains. Is it to try to ensure we lay a solid foundation of truth on which to build our Christian lives? Is it to highlight the things which are important, to help us avoid getting caught up in rigid dogma where we should, in fact, be far more flexible? Or is it to guard ourselves from heresy such as those peddled by the Christian cults?

All of these are good reasons, but above them all is the fact that what we believe shapes how we live – as such it is important to remind ourselves of the things we believe to ensure these are the things that shape our lives. The Creed doesn't waste time with the less important matters, but focuses only on things that are essential – the areas of Christian belief that we are to grip firmly and immovably. Here then, we have the core truths of Christianity laid out for us – the beliefs that, above all else, should shape the way we live our lives as God's people.

I believe in God, the Father, Almighty, creator of heaven and earth.

I believe in Jesus Christ, his only Son, our Lord. He was conceived by the Holy Spirit, born of the Virgin Mary, suffered under Pontius Pilate, was crucified, died, and was buried; he descended to the dead.

On the third day he rose again; he ascended into heaven, he is seated at the right hand of the Father, and he will come to judge the living and the dead.

I believe in the Holy Spirit, the holy catholic Church, the communion of saints, the forgiveness of sins, the resurrection of the body, and the life everlasting.

WEEK 1

I Believe in One God

Opening Icebreaker

Many cultures around the world have, or at least had, a host of different deities, each playing a distinct role. For example, Thor was the Norse god of thunder and warfare, Erebos was the Greek god of darkness, and Coyolxauhqui (pronounced 'Co-hol-SHAW-ki') was the Aztec goddess of the moon.

How many such gods and goddesses can you think of, and what were their areas of responsibility?

Bible Readings

- Genesis 1:1
- Deuteronomy 6:4–5
- Psalm 14:1
- Isaiah 46:8–11
- 1 John 3:1

Creed Statement

I believe in God, the Father, Almighty, creator of heaven and earth.

Opening Our Eyes

'Hear, O Israel: The LORD our God, the LORD is one.'
(Deut. 6:4)

When Moses spoke these words to the Israelites it was
to remind them that they were different. They had left
Egypt with their pantheon of gods, and the promised
land lay before them, filled with even more gods. The
Israelites needed to remember that they worshipped the
one, true God.

The Creed opens with a declaration of belief in God,
and the writer to the Hebrews said, 'anyone who comes
to [God] must believe that he exists' (Heb. 11:6). But
our belief is not simply in divine beings in general. The
Nicene Creed includes the word 'one' – we believe not in
many gods, but in 'one God'. And let's face it, this is much
easier than having lots of gods and goddesses for different
areas of life. 'Want your crops to grow? You need to pray
to that god.' 'Having trouble at work? You need to offer
a sacrifice to this goddess.' That said, we don't believe in
one God because it is easier, but because the Bible tells
us, 'The LORD is one'.

It also tells us that this one God is our Father. Back in
the ancient world, kings would sometimes take the title of
'father' to imply:
• principality – the king had headship over the people
• provision – the king would ensure his people had all
  they needed to survive
• protection – the king would keep his people safe.

Certainly these three things are true of God. He is the
principal over all, sovereign of everything. He is the
provider, giving us all that we need. And He is our
protector. But when Jesus called God, 'Our Father'

(Matt. 6:9), He was talking about something even more amazing. He was talking about a relationship – a loving relationship with God as our Father and us as His children. And those of us who have put our faith in Him *really are* His children, 'born', as John wrote, 'not of natural descent ... but born of God' (John 1:13).

Kings would also use the title 'father' to imply power, and the Creed refers to God as 'Almighty'. When this word is used in the Bible it does not necessarily suggest the ability to do anything whatsoever – after all, 'it is impossible for God to lie' (Heb. 6:18). Rather they suggest an ability to do what you desire. The Hebrew term 'El Shaddai', usually translated 'God Almighty', really means 'God, who is sufficient'. He is Almighty in that His power is sufficient for His purpose, or as He puts it, 'What I have said, that I will bring about; what I have planned, that I will do' (Isa. 46:11).

This is great news for us since it means that God is able to fulfil all the promises laid out in Scripture, no matter how fantastic they may seem. Not only *able*, but He *will* fulfil His promises!

As if to illustrate this, the Creed ends with the declaration that God created the heavens and the earth. 'The heavens declare the glory of God;' wrote David, 'the skies proclaim the work of his hands' (Psa. 19:1). And Paul stated that, 'since the creation of the world God's invisible qualities ... have been clearly seen, being understood from what has been made' (Rom. 1:20). If we are ever in any doubt that there is a God, the world around us, even our own existence – even the existence of those who say there is no God! – is our proof that He *does* exist.

Discussion Starters

1. Psalm 14:1 says, 'The fool says in his heart, "There is no God"' and yet there are many atheists we would consider intelligent, even wise. Why do you think people choose not to believe, or even cannot believe, in God?

   _____

   _____

   _____

   _____

2. Why do you believe there is a God, and what difference does this fundamental belief make to your life?

   So much evidence

   No one has ever made anything from nothing

   Witness & Testamony

   _____

3. Read Isaiah 46:10–11 and Romans 8:31. How might statements such as these be affected if there was not only one God, but many gods, such as those worshipped in Ancient Rome?

   _____

   _____

   _____

   _____

   _____

4. Read 1 John 3:1. How does it make a difference to your life knowing God as your Father?

   _____

   _____

   _____

   _____

5. What promises have you had from God, either in the Bible or personally? How does knowing that His power is sufficient for His purposes shape your thinking about those promises?

Answer to prayer i.e. house

6. What suggestions have you come across explaining how God created the heavens and the earth? Does it matter what you believe about the method of creation?

Belief in God the Creator — most important

7. If you were asked by an atheist friend why you believe in God, how would you answer?

Evidence in Bible & so much history
Help in hard times.

Belief in Action

Terms like God, Almighty and creator can seem somewhat irrelevant to daily life – they are so grand and abstract it can be hard to ground such concepts. But the point of the Creed is not to reel off objective facts, but to help us grasp truths that should shape our lives.

Although these terms are indeed grand and somewhat abstract, when we consider that they apply to the One we call 'Father', with whom we have been granted an intimate, loving relationship, suddenly the objective facts become wonderful, personal, life-changing truths.

If we really believe that there is a God, a single being who created the heavens, the earth and everything in it, and who rules over them, then the whole purpose of our lives must surely be given over to seeking Him and must be lived in complete devotion and service to Him.

If we really believe that God is our Father, who has brought us into His family, then we must surely live as though we are His children – 'And that is what we are!' (1 John 3:1) – following His teaching on how best to live, and coming to Him with confidence even when we mess up.

And if we really believe that God is Almighty, that He is able to do what He says He will do, then we will trust Him no matter what life in this fallen world throws at us. And we will come to Him with our requests, because He alone has the power to do as He desires.

WEEK 2

I Believe Jesus is God

Opening Icebreaker

The fact that our beliefs shape how we live is true in all areas of life. In fact I don't think it would be too much of a stretch to say everything we do stems from what we believe.

For example, I eat, work and exercise (occasionally) because I *believe* these things are important; I use the postal service and internet banking because I *believe* they are safe; and I don't stick my fingers in the electric sockets or walk in front of moving vehicles because I *believe* it would be detrimental to my health.

Think of some of the things you choose to do, or not to do, and work out on what beliefs they are based.

Bible Readings

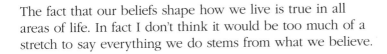

- Mark 14:61–64
- John 1:1
- John 10:30–33
- Colossians 1:15–18
- Revelation 1:8, 22:13

Creed Statement

I believe in Jesus Christ, [God's] only Son, our Lord.

Opening Our Eyes

There is surely no one who has been the subject of more controversy than Jesus. This is hardly surprising, since He is also the most famous and most talked about person who has ever lived – the subject of over twenty-five million internet searches every month! And the main controversy revolves around who He is.

Although few seriously question the historical existence of Jesus, most people consider Him nothing more than a human. They may credit Him as being a good person, like Ghandi or Mother Teresa, but the idea that He is God is unthinkable.

The Apostles' Creed however calls Jesus, 'Christ' – the Messiah, a divine figure prophesied about in the Old Testament. And it calls Him 'Lord', a title which the Jews used (and still do today) in place of the name of God, 'YHWH'.

The Nicene Creed is even clearer, referring to Jesus as, 'God from God, light from light, true God from true God … of one Being with the Father'. So, is Jesus God?

To answer this we could look at statements from Paul's letters such as, 'by [Jesus] all things were created: things in heaven and on earth, visible and invisible … all things were created by him and for him' (Col. 1:16), or his reference to Jesus as, 'being in very nature God' (Phil. 2:6), and 'our great God and Saviour' (Titus 2:13).

We could go to the writer to the Hebrews, who called Jesus, 'the radiance of God's glory and the exact representation of his being' (Heb. 1:3).

We could go to John's Gospel, which begins, 'In the beginning was the Word, and the Word was with God, and the Word was God' (John 1:1), or Peter's second letter, whose opening statement refers to, 'our God and Saviour Jesus Christ' (2 Pet. 1:1).

But the best place to go is to Jesus Himself. After all, many people believe that Jesus never claimed to be God. But what about His claim that, 'I and the Father are one' (John 10:30)? His Jewish hearers obviously took this as a claim to be God since they immediately tried to stone Him, saying, 'you, a mere man, claim to be God' (v33).

In John 8 there is a similar scenario when Jesus tells the Jews, 'before Abraham was born, I am!' (v58). Again the Jews started reaching for stones to silence this blasphemy because the phrase 'I am' had a special meaning to them; they believed it was related to God's name (see Exodus 3), making this a claim to be God.

This wasn't the only time He used this phrase. Consider these 'I am' claims of Jesus, noting also how outrageous they would be if made by a mere human:
• 'I am the Bread of life' (John 6:35)
• 'I am the Light of the World' (John 8:12)
• 'I am the good shepherd' (John 10:11)
• 'I am the resurrection and the life' (John 11:25)
• 'I am the way and the truth and the life' (John 14:6)
• 'I am the First and the Last. I am the Living One' (Rev. 1:17–18)
• 'I am the Alpha and the Omega' (Rev. 22:13).

And at His trial, when asked if He was the Messiah, Jesus responded, 'I am' (Mark 14:62), and for this claim to be God they sentenced Him to death!

To suggest that Jesus never claimed to be God is to simply ignore the wealth of biblical evidence. Jesus not only clearly claimed to be God, but He was crucified for it. This is why we believe Jesus *is* God.

Discussion Starters

1. When you think of Jesus, do you tend to imagine Him more as a man or God? Why do you think this is?

_____

_____

_____

_____

_____

2. Consider the customary claim that Jesus was 'just a good man'. How does that stand up in light of the evidence of His life?

_____

_____

_____

_____

_____

3. Jesus tends to be a highly controversial figure. Why do you think so many people are eager to argue against Jesus' divinity?

_____

_____

_____

_____

_____

4. Compare Revelation 1:8 and 22:13. How do these verses clearly claim that Jesus is God? Can you think of others?

_____

_____

_____

_____

_____

5. Many people consider that the argument over Jesus' divinity is pointless. Why does it matter that Jesus is God?

_____

_____

_____

_____

_____

6. What difference does the belief that Jesus is God make to your life, both on a grand scale and on a daily basis?

_____

_____

_____

_____

_____

7. Jehovah's Witnesses do not believe Jesus is God. If they came knocking at your door, how would you explain your belief that He is God?

_____

_____

_____

_____

_____

Belief in Action

The question of whether or not Jesus is God may appear to be little more than a philosophical irrelevance; but, of course, this is not the case. The Creed takes great care to ensure that this point is clear. It is one of the fundamental things we believe and in which we put our faith. And since real, saving faith shapes the way we think and speak and act – since it affects the way we live – the fact that Jesus is God should make a difference to our lives.

If we really believe that Jesus is God the Son, God's only Son, then, as we saw in the first session, our lives must surely be lived in complete devotion and service to Him. We should pay great attention to the things He said – His teachings that have been recorded for us in the Gospels. As the writer to the Hebrews wrote in his opening statement, 'In the past God spoke to our ancestors through the prophets at many times and in various ways, but in these last days he has spoken to us by his Son, whom he appointed heir of all things, and through whom he made the universe' (Heb. 1:1–2).

And if we really believed that Jesus is our Lord, the one to whom we have devoted our lives, we would apply those teachings to our daily lives, demonstrating our reverence and our love for Him. As Jesus said, 'Anyone who loves me will obey my teaching' (John 14:23).

WEEK 3

I Believe Jesus is Human

Opening Icebreaker

Here's a little memory test for you, based on the classic 'I went to the market' game. The first person says, 'I know that I'm a human, because …' then names something that makes them human.

The next person takes up the refrain, 'I know that I'm a human, because …' giving the first person's reason and then adding their own. This continues round the group with each person recounting the reasons given so far before adding their own. If a person cannot remember what came before, or cannot think of a reason, they are 'out'.

Bible Readings

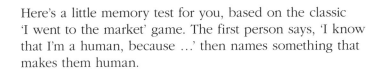

- Luke 2:40
- John 1:14
- Philippians 2:5–8
- Hebrews 4:15
- 1 John 1:1

Creed Statement

He was conceived by the Holy Spirit, born of the Virgin Mary, suffered under Pontius Pilate, was crucified, died, and was buried; he descended to the dead.

Opening Our Eyes

It is not only Jesus' divinity that has come under attack. There have been those who deny His humanity as well, claiming Jesus only seemed to be human or that God 'possessed' the body of a man during His time on earth. To combat such teaching, the Nicene Creed added the phrase 'and was made man'. Yes, He was conceived by the Holy Spirit, which may seem rather mystic and non-human, but He was also 'born of the Virgin Mary'.

I've been present at the births of all four of my children, and it's about as human as it gets, with lots of pushing, shouting and pain, and then suddenly that huge bump turns into a tiny, helpless human. Jesus went through that very process!

Luke tells us that Jesus didn't stay a baby but 'grew and became strong' (Luke 2:40). He had a normal, human body, just like us. He must have had eyes, because He looked with them. He must have had a mouth because He spoke and Mark tells us He even spat in a blind man's eyes! He must have had a tongue because He tasted with it, and ears, because He heard people speak. John tells us Jesus had legs and feet and used them to walk, because, being a human, He couldn't be everywhere at once. Mark informs us Jesus had arms and fingers, which He used to touch people just as people touched Him, because his body was real, not just an illusion.

In addition to this physical evidence, we see that Jesus also felt the natural desires of having a human body: He got hungry and ate, He got thirsty and drank, and He got tired and slept. Our bodies have these desires too, because we are human, just like Jesus.

Finally Jesus had feelings and emotions consistent with being a human. He was astonished by people's faith (or lack of it). He felt compassion. He got angry and distressed, sorrowful and troubled. He suffered anguish and wept, but also experienced joy. Hebrews tells us that Jesus was 'tempted in every way, just as we are' (Heb. 4:15), and while James 1:13 says that God cannot be tempted, we know that humans can, and by becoming human Jesus opened Himself up to all the weaknesses and conflicts that come with being human, including temptation.

The Creed says that Jesus 'suffered under Pontius Pilate', mentioning the Roman Procurator by name to show that Jesus was a real person, who existed in history. Under Pontius Pilate, Jesus was subjected to the most horrific treatment, and because He was human, Jesus experienced it all just as we might. They flogged Him. His face was punched and slapped. His head was beaten with a stick and pierced with thorns. They drove nails through His hands, pinning Him to the cross, and ultimately, as we humans do, Jesus died.

John is often pointed to as the writer who stressed Jesus' divinity, but he was also eager to stress His humanity. Referring to Jesus, he wrote, 'The Word became flesh and made his dwelling among us' (John 1:14), and 'That which was from the beginning, which we have heard, which we have seen with our eyes, which we have looked at and our hands have touched' (1 John 1:1).

Jesus is not simply an invented character to teach us moral principles, nor some mystic, timeless entity. Jesus really is the human Son of God.

Discussion Starters

1. Why do you think it was necessary for Jesus to become human?

2. Read about Jesus' human attributes in the verses on page 19. Why might people be unconvinced that Jesus is human despite these statements?

3. What difference does the belief that Jesus became human and experienced life in this fallen world make to your life?

4. If Jesus only seemed to be human or was some kind of super-human, why would that make a difference?

5. Read 1 Corinthians 15:20–25. How does it feel to know that a human is sitting on the throne, ruling over the physical and spiritual realms?

_____

_____

_____

_____

_____

6. The Creed refers to Jesus as 'Lord'. Although this is not a common title in everyday use, what does it mean to you? How is Jesus' lordship demonstrated in your life?

_____

_____

_____

_____

_____

7. If you were faced with someone who believed Jesus was not, and is not, a real human, how would you explain your belief in His humanity?

_____

_____

_____

_____

_____

Belief in Action

It can be all too easy to become blasé about the idea that God became human. After all, people go on about it every year at Christmas, throwing around the word 'incarnate' like it's going out of fashion (which it probably is). But when you actually stop and think about it, it's mind-blowing. God, who created the whole universe and everything in it, actually became a real human being, with a body just like ours. If that's not a belief that should shape how we live, nothing is.

If we really believe that Jesus became human, experiencing what it is like to live in this fallen world, then, as the writer to the Hebrews says, 'we do not have a high priest who is unable to sympathise with our weaknesses, but we have one who has been tempted in every way, just as we are' (Heb. 4:15). He knows what it is like to be tempted, to be hungry and thirsty, to be in pain and weary, to be hurt and abandoned by others. He knows what it is like to suffer just like us. This knowledge should help us to draw near to Him in our own suffering and temptation.

And if we really believe that a human is sitting on the throne and ruling over all things, it shows us the great value God has placed in humanity – so much so that He became human. This will spur us on to loving our fellow humans, reaching out to those who do not yet know Him.

If Jesus was not a real human then He could not know what it is like to suffer in this world; nor could He have offered Himself as a sacrifice on behalf of humanity. We would have no saviour and no hope. Thankfully the Bible and the Creed are clear: Jesus really is a human!

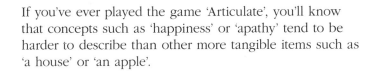

WEEK 4

I Believe in the Holy Spirit

Opening Icebreaker

If you've ever played the game 'Articulate', you'll know that concepts such as 'happiness' or 'apathy' tend to be harder to describe than other more tangible items such as 'a house' or 'an apple'.

Take turns describing a concept to the rest of the group, who will try to guess what the concept is. The description must not contain the word(s) you are describing.

For example, if I was trying to describe 'loneliness' I might say, 'It's an unpleasant feeling you get when you are apart from people you know'.

I have suggested a few concepts to describe in the Leader's Notes on page 56.

Bible Readings

- Genesis 1:2
- Psalm 139:7–9
- John 14:26, 16:13–15
- 1 Corinthians 6:19–20
- 2 Corinthians 13:14

Creed Statement

I believe in the Holy Spirit.

Opening Our Eyes

The Apostles' Creed delivers a short, simple statement about the Holy Spirit. And it's a true statement – we *do* believe in the Holy Spirit. But what exactly do we believe?

I once asked a group of teenage Christians what images came to their minds at the mention of the Holy Spirit. The responses ranged from 'mist' and 'clouds' to 'some kind of energy force, like in Stars Wars, that represents God's power'. Not one of them, however, suggested that the Holy Spirit is either God Himself or a person. Such responses are unfortunately common, even among adult believers.

This confusion no doubt springs from the Holy Spirit's association in the Bible with such inanimate entities as wind, water, fire and oil. But these are merely pictures to help us understand something about the Holy Spirit. They are not meant to be taken any more literally than the description of Jesus as a gate (John 10:7) – it tells us something about Him, but no one believes Jesus really was an actual gate!

The Nicene Creed expands on that simple statement, describing the Holy Spirit as 'The Lord, the giver of life, who proceeds from the Father and the Son. With the Father and the Son he is worshipped and glorified.' It is clear then that we do not believe He is an inanimate entity, but a person – God Himself.

When I say we believe He is a person, I don't mean that He is human. But He is a person all the same. Consider the fact that Jesus said the Holy Spirit would 'guide you into all truth. He will not speak on his own; he will speak only what he hears, and he will tell you what is yet to come' (John 16:13). Guide, speak and tell. As a rule, inanimate objects like houses and apples do not do these things – only a person does. Consider these other

descriptions of the Holy Spirit:
* He knows the thoughts of God (1 Cor. 2:10)
* He prays on our behalf and helps us to pray
  (Rom. 8:26)
* He has a will (1 Cor. 12:11)
* He can be grieved (Eph. 4:30)
* He has intelligence and goodness (Neh. 9:20)
* He loves (Rom. 15:30).

Such things can only be said about a person.

As for believing He is God, this is something on which
we tend to be more clear. The writer to the Hebrews
talks about the 'eternal Spirit' (Heb. 9:14), and only
God is eternal. David wrote about the Holy Spirit being
inescapable, because He is everywhere (Psa. 139:7,9), and
only God is everywhere. In Acts 5, Peter admonishes
Ananias for lying to the Holy Spirit saying, 'You have not
lied just to human beings but to God' (v4). Paul refers to
our bodies as, 'a temple of the Holy Spirit' (1 Cor. 6:19),
when earlier in the same letter he calls us 'God's temple'
(1 Cor 3:16). And in John's Gospel, he records Jesus'
conversation with Nicodemus about being 'born of the
Spirit' (John 3:8), yet in the opening chapter he calls us
children 'born of God' (John 1:13).

So, then, we believe not in some abstract, impersonal
entity, but in the Holy Spirit, who is God Himself, who
loves us and lives in us. It is not, 'may the Force be with
you', but may 'the fellowship of the Holy Spirit be with
you' (2 Cor. 13:14)!

Discussion Starters

1. What image comes to mind when you hear the phrase, 'the Holy Spirit'?

2. Read John 3:8, Acts 2:3–4 and 1 Corinthians 12:13. What do these pictures of the Holy Spirit as wind, water and fire tell us about Him and what He does?

3. Why might such pictures distract people from thinking about the Holy Spirit as God Himself?

4. What do you understand by the phrase, 'filled with the Holy Spirit'?

5. What tasks does the Holy Spirit peform in the life of God's people, according to the Bible?

_____

_____

_____

_____

_____

6. Read 1 Corinthians 6:19 and 2 Timothy 1:14. What difference does your belief that the Holy Spirit lives in you make to your daily life?

_____

_____

_____

_____

_____

7. How would you explain to a Christian who thinks of the Holy Spirit as some sort of cosmic force that the Holy Spirit is a person – God Himself?

_____

_____

_____

_____

_____

Belief in Action

'I will ask the Father, and he will give you another advocate to be with you forever – the Spirit of truth' (John 14:16–17).

The Holy Spirit has been sent to be with God's people. More than that, He is *in* us – our bodies are temples of the Holy Spirit (1 Cor. 6:19). Now, if the Holy Spirit is just some sort of impersonal, cosmic energy force or merely a symbol of God's power, this is not all that comforting. Yet the Bible is clear that the Holy Spirit is a person, and not just any person, but God Himself. Just consider this statement that all Christians can make: 'God lives in me.' That is a staggering revelation and one which, if we believe it, will shape every moment of our daily lives. Remember that Jesus said the Holy Spirit would guide us, teach us and tell us what is to come.

If we really believe that the Holy Spirit lives in us, we will find ourselves increasingly looking to Him for guidance in all that we think, say and do – no matter how big or small – knowing that His leading is best and that He deals with us personally because He is a person. We would be diligent in learning to recognise His voice so that we can be sure of when He is speaking to us. And we would have complete confidence in all situations, good and bad, because we are assured that God is with us at all times.

What a wonderful thing it is to believe in the Holy Spirit, the Lord, the Giver of life – God in us.

WEEK 5

I Believe in the Church

Opening Icebreaker

There are at least seven legitimate definitions for the word 'church' in the English language. For example, if I said 'every Wednesday our church is used by a ballroom dancing class to do ... er, ballroom dancing', the word 'church' here would be referring to the physical church building.

What other meanings for the word 'church' can you think of, giving examples of each?

Bible Readings

- Matthew 16:19
- Matthew 28:19
- 1 Corinthians 12:14–20
- Ephesians 2:19–22
- 1 Peter 2:9–10

Creed Statement

I believe in ... the holy catholic Church, the communion of saints.

Opening Our Eyes

Around the world today the Church is split into thousands of denominations, many the result of schisms and disagreements. As such it may not be immediately clear what the Apostles' Creed is referring to when it talks about 'the Church'. Certainly it is talking about people rather than buildings, but which people exactly?

When the Council of Nicea met with the aim of uniting the groups of Christians that had been scattered during the centuries of persecution, they faced this same question. They answered it by adding to the Church's description as 'one' and 'Apostolic'.

The fact that the Church is 'one' is of huge importance. Consider Paul's words to the church in Corinth, that the body is a unit, 'but all its many parts form one body' (1 Cor. 12:12). Our bodies are made up of lots of different bits, but we don't wake in the morning and have to hunt under the covers to find where our ears or a lung have wandered off to in the night – our bodies are a single, connected entity. The same is true of the Church. No matter how it may appear today, the Church is one body, incorporating every single follower of Christ, and one day we will all live together as the united people of God … forever!

So who exactly is included in this one Church? The Apostles' Creed describes the Church as 'holy' and 'the communion of the saints' – the joining together of those who are holy. This word, 'holy', is often thought of as meaning 'pure' or 'godly', but that's not entirely accurate. In Exodus 30, God warns Moses about the use of holy oil saying, 'Do not pour it on anyone else's body and do not make any oil using the same formula … Whoever [does so] must be cut off from their people' (vv32–33). The oil was holy, set apart, to be used only for a specific, godly purpose. This is the essence of what it means to be 'holy'. That which is holy is set apart – it belongs to God and is only to be used for godly purposes.

Consider these descriptions of Christians:
- '... you are no longer foreigners and strangers, but fellow citizens with God's people' (Eph. 2:19)
- '... you are a chosen people, a royal priesthood, a holy nation, God's special possession' (1 Pet. 2:9).

Jesus said 'I will build my church' (Matt. 16:18) and He builds it with those He has purchased with His life, who have put their faith in Him. Such people belong to God and are therefore holy, set apart for Him. *This* is why we are to be pure and godly.

The Creed also describes the Church as 'catholic', which can cause confusion for some; after all, we usually only come across this word when talking about the Roman Catholic church. But they do not have the monopoly on this word any more than the Eastern Orthodox church does on the word 'orthodox', or the Church of England does on the word 'England'.

'Catholic' simply means 'universal' or 'general' and has to do with the Church's diversity and breadth. Jesus told His followers to 'go and make disciples of all nations' (Matt. 28:19). As the Church has spread, it has crossed boundaries of race, class, culture, world-view and time. The Church is 'catholic' in that it embraces this diversity without seeking to fit everyone into a standard Christian mould – unity without uniformity.

Discussion Starters

1. Why do you think there are so many different Church denominations around the world today, and what impact might this have on the unity of God's people?

_____

_____

_____

_____

_____

2. How would you explain the meaning of the Creed's phrase, 'the communion of the saints'?

_____

_____

_____

_____

_____

3. What do you believe about the Church, and what difference has this belief made to your daily life?

_____

_____

_____

_____

_____

4. Read Ephesians 5:22–33. Although Paul's primary focus here is on marriage, what do these verses tell us about the Church?

_____

_____

_____

_____

_____

5. What do you understand by the terms 'catholic' and 'apostolic', as used in the Creed to refer to the Church?

_____

_____

_____

_____

_____

6. How do you and those in your local church live out the call to be 'holy'?

_____

_____

_____

_____

_____

7. If you had a friend in a denomination which taught that they alone were the 'true Church', how would you explain to them the biblical definition of the Church?

_____

_____

_____

_____

_____

Belief in Action

'... just as each of us has one body with many members, and these members do not all have the same function, so in Christ we, though many, form one body, and each member belongs to all the others' (Rom. 12:4–5).

While we tend to be clear that the Church is the people of God, we do not always live out this reality. Even in our own local churches we can sometimes find ourselves looking down on those in other churches because they do things differently or their beliefs on secondary issues are different to ours. However, the Bible is clear that all those who have put their faith in Jesus, and who believe those things that truly matter – as laid out for us in the Creed – are part of the Church.

If we really believe that the Church is one, this will shape our interaction with other believers, both in our local churches and in the Church in general. Such a belief will help us to overcome disagreements and divisions and even the natural dislikes we may have for others in the Church.

If we really believe that the Church is holy – the community of the saints – it will spur us on to live 'as foreigners and exiles, to abstain from sinful desires' (1 Pet. 2:11) and live instead for God's glory.

If we really believe the Church is catholic, in that it embraces the diversity of many cultures and practices, this will make us more accepting of other churches rather than judging them for being different.

And if we really believe the Church is apostolic – that it is built on the teaching of the Apostles, on the absolute authority of the Scriptures – this will ensure that we cling to these fundamental truths and are open-handed about secondary issues rather than falling out over them.

WEEK 6

I Believe in Salvation

Opening Icebreaker

My children love playing the card game Go Fish – it has everything you could possibly want in a game: guesswork, suspense, chance, skill and the opportunity to shout 'go fish!' at people. Why not play Go Fish as a group? For the rules, see the Leader's Notes section for Week 6 at the back of the book.

Bible Readings

- Genesis 2:17
- John 3:16
- Ephesians 5:23
- Philippians 2:5–8
- 1 Peter 3:18

Creed Statement

On the third day [Jesus] rose again; he ascended into heaven, he is seated at the right hand of the Father, and he will come to judge the living and the dead.

I believe in … the forgiveness of sins.

Opening Our Eyes

The word 'save' can be used in many different contexts. For example, in the Icebreaker the aim was to save up matching cards, but if I was looking to buy a new car, I would be saving money instead. Neither example has anything to do with Christian salvation, but they do show us the five key principles of salvation:

1. There is a person doing the saving – the 'saver' or 'saviour'.

2. There is an object that is saved – cards or money, in the above examples.

3. There is something the object is saved *from* – the cards from being obtained by others, or the money from being spent.

4. The person saving has to do something – collect the cards or earn the money.

5. There is a goal for all this saving – winning the game or buying the car.

As we consider Christian salvation, the identity of the person doing the saving is well known. In Ephesians 5, Paul wrote, 'Christ is the head of the church, his body, of which he is the Saviour' (Eph. 5:23).

So what about the object being saved? And what exactly is it being saved from?

While the Apostles' Creed does not specifically mention the word 'salvation', the Nicene Creed, when talking about Jesus, adds the phrase, 'who for us men and for our salvation came down from heaven'. Jesus came to earth to save people – men and women like us. But in order to see what He came to save us *from*, we need to go back a little further. Back to the beginning, in fact.

Having created everything and declared it to be 'very good', God gave the man He had created one rule: 'you must not eat from the tree of the knowledge of good and evil, for when you eat from it you will certainly die' (Gen. 2:17). When Adam disobeyed this rule, he willingly chose to break his relationship with God, becoming instead His enemy, condemned to death.

As the Old Testament unfolds we see God's desire for that relationship to be restored. He called the Israelites to be His people, drawing near to them in the Tabernacle and giving them the Law to help maintain that closeness. Despite this, however, the separation remained. God drew as close as He could, but He was still cut off from His people, hidden away behind a curtain inside a tent.

This is why Jesus 'came down from heaven', becoming human, because it was a human who had severed that relationship with God, so only a human could restore it. That said, in order to restore it fully, an eternal sacrifice needed to be paid for the rebellion against the eternal God. Thankfully, as we have seen, Jesus was not only human, but was also eternal, being God Himself, 'And being found in appearance as a man, he humbled himself and became obedient to death – even death on a cross!' (Phil. 2:8).

So, we know who our Saviour is, and who it is who is being saved – though the Bible is also clear that salvation is specifically for those who trust in Jesus. We have seen what we are saved from, death and separation from God, and we have seen what Jesus had to do to save us.

As for the fifth part, the goal of our salvation, we will consider this in the final session.

Discussion Starters

1. The Bible is clear that we are all counted as sinners because of Adam's disobedience. Why is this the case, and do you think it is fair?

_____

_____

_____

_____

_____

2. The Israelites were God's people and He dwelled in their midst, so why was it necessary for God to be set apart from them in the Holy of Holies?

_____

_____

_____

_____

_____

3. Read John 3:16, Acts 16:30–31 and 2 Thessalonians 2:13. Who receives salvation, and why?

_____

_____

_____

_____

_____

4. Why did Jesus have to suffer and die so that we could receive forgiveness and be granted free access to God?

_____

_____

_____

_____

_____

5. Read Psalm 103:12 and 1 John 1:9. How does it feel to know that your sins have been forgiven, regardless of how unforgivable they may seem to you?

    _____

    _____

    _____

    _____

6. What difference does your belief that God has forgiven your sins make to your life on both a grand scale and on a daily basis?

    _____

    _____

    _____

    _____

7. If you were faced with an interested unbeliever, who had no previous knowledge of Christianity, how would you explain your belief in salvation to them?

    _____

    _____

    _____

    _____

Belief in Action

'... Christ also suffered once for sins, the righteous for the unrighteous, to bring you to God' (1 Pet. 3:18).

This is why Jesus came to earth, becoming human and allowing Himself to be tortured and nailed to the cross – not just so that we could be forgiven, though that is wonderful beyond words, but to bring us to God. Thanks to Jesus we are now able to come to God, to love and be loved by Him. This is earth shattering stuff that, if we truly believe it, will change everything about our lives and the way we live.

If we really believe that Jesus suffered and died for us, this will not only humble us but it will, at the same time, help us to see just how much God loves us. It will also spur us on to share the Gospel with as many others as possible.

If we really believe that we are now free to enter into a loving relationship with God, then, no matter how important a connection we have with anyone else, this relationship will take the highest priority in our lives.

If we really believe that we have been forgiven for our sin, for every thought, word and action that has not been honouring to God, it will help us to forgive others when they sin against us. No matter how devastating and despicable that sin, it cannot begin to compare with all that God has forgiven us.

And if we really believe these things then we can be certain that we are among those who have been saved, and that when Jesus comes again 'to judge the living and the dead', He will declare us righteous.

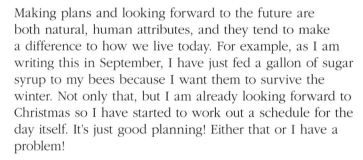

WEEK 7

I Believe in Eternal Life

Opening Icebreaker

Making plans and looking forward to the future are both natural, human attributes, and they tend to make a difference to how we live today. For example, as I am writing this in September, I have just fed a gallon of sugar syrup to my bees because I want them to survive the winter. Not only that, but I am already looking forward to Christmas so I have started to work out a schedule for the day itself. It's just good planning! Either that or I have a problem!

Share other ways that making plans and looking forward to the future might make a difference to how you live today.

Bible Readings

- Genesis 1:31
- Luke 24:36–43
- John 3:16
- 1 Corinthians 15:13–26
- Revelation 21:1–5

Creed Statement

I believe in … the resurrection of the body, and the life everlasting.

Opening Our Eyes

On 12 October 1989 I first realised that I was going to die. I don't think it was because I was in any immediate danger, though my mother was driving me to school at the time so I cannot be certain of that, but I can clearly recall feeling an overwhelming sense of dread and fear at the idea of death.

While dying is one thing that all people have in common, it's not something we enjoy thinking about, much less talking about. Even among Christians this *is* true, because death just seems wrong, somehow. And it is wrong. It's not the way things were meant to be. If Adam had not disobeyed God, he would still be alive today instead of dying at the youthful age of 960! Yet his rebellion and rejection of God led not only to his own death but also ensured the death of every member of the human race, including mine and yours.

All religions seek to tackle this problem, or at least to tackle the issue of what happens next. The Hindus, for example, teach that people are reincarnated according to how they have lived in this life. Even humanists have something to say on the matter, though they believe that we simply cease to exist.

So what about us? What do we believe?

In the previous session, we saw that Jesus died so that we could receive forgiveness for our sin. Thanks to Him we can come to God, with confidence, as children coming to their loving Father. And yet we still die. The Bible tells us that, after death, those who have trusted in Jesus and received that forgiveness, 'will be with [Him] in paradise' (Luke 23:43) – an entirely spiritual existence. And yet, in the beginning, God created the physical universe for us to live in together, declaring it, 'very good' (Gen. 1:31). We were made for a spiritual *and* physical existence and it is just such a future that we are looking forward to.

As the Creed states, Jesus 'rose again' with a real, physical body – one which was able to be touched and to eat (Luke 24:39–43). Paul said, in a chapter devoted to resurrection, that Jesus is just 'the firstfruits of those who have fallen asleep' (1 Cor. 15:20) and elsewhere he wrote, 'just as Christ was raised from the dead ... we too may live a new life' (Rom. 6:4).

'I am the resurrection and the life,' said Jesus, 'The one who believes in me will live, even though they die' (John 11:25). This is the resurrection of the dead, the day when *all* people will receive new physical bodies like His. However, only those who have received the forgiveness that we read about in the previous session will receive everlasting life.

So what is life after death going to be like? I remember thinking it involved floating around on clouds, strumming harps and suchlike, which, to be honest, sounded pretty boring – hardly an eternity to look forward to! But the reality is much more exciting: the life everlasting is the fulfilment of God's original plan. The closing chapters of the Bible speak of 'a new heaven and a new earth' (Rev. 21:1), a restoration of this physical world, where we will live with God, loving Him and one another in perfection forever. This is the goal of our salvation, and it's a future that's really worth believing in!

Discussion Starters

1. As Christians, we tend to refer to life after death as 'going to heaven', while being somewhat vague about what this involves. What do you believe will happen when we die?

    _____

    _____

    _____

    _____

    _____

2. Since 'the life everlasting' is God's goal for humanity, why do you think He doesn't simply take us to be with Him the instant we believe?

    _____

    _____

    _____

    _____

    _____

3. Read Isaiah 66:17–24 and Revelation 21:1–5. How has the belief in eternal life after death shaped the way you live?

    _____

    _____

    _____

    _____

    _____

4. Read 1 Corinthians 15:19. How might you live differently if you didn't believe in life after death?

    _____

    _____

    _____

    _____

5. 'Misthology' is the fancy theological term used to describe the doctrine of rewards – the Bible's teaching that the things we do in this life can earn rewards for our eternal life. What is your opinion on storing up such treasure in heaven?

_____

_____

_____

_____

_____

6. How would you answer somebody who asked you what the difference was between reincarnation and resurrection?

_____

_____

_____

_____

7. How would you explain the resurrection of the dead and the life everlasting to a humanist, who believed that *this* life is all there is?

_____

_____

_____

_____

_____

Belief in Action

'But in keeping with his promise we are looking forward to a new heaven and a new earth, where righteousness dwells. So ... make every effort to be found spotless, blameless and at peace with him' (2 Pet. 3:13–14).

Our belief in everlasting life should not be restricted to that future life alone, but should shape the way we life our lives here and now. Consider what the writer to the Hebrews said about Moses: 'He chose to be ill-treated along with the people of God rather than to enjoy the fleeting pleasures of sin ... because he was looking ahead to his reward' (Heb. 11:25–26). This is what Jesus was talking about in the Sermon on the Mount, where He told His followers to, 'store up for yourselves treasures in heaven, where moths and vermin do not destroy, and where thieves do not break in and steal' (Matt. 6:20). When we live our lives for God, doing those things which please and glorify Him, we are storing up heavenly treasure, looking forward to our eternal future despite the cost in the present. Regardless of whether the idea of receiving rewards appeals to you, the Bible presents this as an important incentive for godly living!

So if we really believe in eternal life – the promise of a new, perfect world where we will live together with Him in new, perfect bodies – we will pursue God now, increasingly living our lives for Him, loving one another, battling temptation and sharing the good news of all that Jesus has provided for us. These things are hard now, but we do them because we believe a day is coming when the godly way of life will be the only way of life, and we will live together with Him forever!

Leader's Notes

These notes are designed to help you lead these sessions in a group. Please do read through the notes before each session to help with your preparation. It is also worth reading through the Belief in Action section to get a feel for the overall message of the session.

Week 1: I Believe in One God

This first session focuses on the opening statement of the Apostles' Creed, which professes faith in God as our almighty Father, who created all things.

Opening Icebreaker

Apart from breaking the ice, these group exercises are supposed to get people to start thinking about the topic, or at least something relating to it.

The icebreaker for this first session considers the idea of worshipping many gods and goddesses.

Bible Readings

All the sessions in this book have a number of verses that relate to the topic. It is not necessary to read these together as a group as they are most often used in the discussion starters.

Creed Statement

Each session relates to a statement of belief from the
Apostles' Creed. The statement in question is quoted here.

Discussion Starters

As the name suggests, these are questions to help start
group discussions. Feel free to use as many or as few of
these as necessary, and add to them as you feel led. In
these Leader's Notes I will give you background to the
questions I have written for each session, which may help
you lead the times of discussion.

1. To help tackle this Discussion Starter, it may be worth
reading through Romans 1:18–25 as this talks about the fact
that the world around us reveals God's existence to everyone
– the problem is that people want to be their own god.

2. This question is concerned *only* with the difference
made by a belief that there is a God. Discussion Starter 4
offers the opportunity to consider how a *relationship* with
God makes a difference. It is worth having an example to
share from your own life to get the discussion going.

3. The point here is that if you have many gods they can
hinder each other and you need the right one for the right
task. No such god could ever have made the claims God
does in these verses.

4. As the aim of this book is to explore how belief shapes
action, each session will include Discussion Starters that
consider how this works out in everyday life. The aim
here is to be as practical as possible so it is worth being
prepared to share a practical way in which your life is
affected by the belief that God is your Father.

5. Some people may be reticent about sharing personal promises from God, but here are some Bible verses with promises for us all, just to get you started: Jeremiah 29:11, Matthew 11:28–29, John 3:16, Romans 8:28, Philippians 4:19, 1 John 1:9, Revelation 22:12.

6. This Discussion Starter could end up going on for a while if you have people with strong opinions on the subject of creation. It may be worth keeping the discussion around the first question brief, before considering the second, more important, question.

The bottom-line here is that the arguments over whether it was a literal six-day creation or took billions of years do not really matter. The fundamental truth is that, whatever the process involved, God made all things.

7. There is a saying, 'you don't really know something unless you can explain it'. Each set of Discussion Starters ends with a question that involves people explaining what they believe. This will help to ensure a clear understanding of what we believe.

It may be worth turning this into a role-playing exercise, with one person playing the atheist and the other explaining their belief in God.

Week 2: I Believe Jesus is God

This session draws on statements from the Apostles' Creed and Nicene Creed that profess faith in the fact that Jesus is God, the son of God.

Opening Icebreaker

The aim of this group exercise is to reinforce the idea that our lives are shaped by our beliefs. I have given a couple of examples of this from everyday life, but it may be worth thinking of some others before the session to help get the ball rolling.

Discussion Starters

1. As Christians, the natural desire is to give the 'right' answer. However, this is not necessarily the true answer, as we will all have a slight skew in one direction or the other. For example, I tend to think of Jesus more as a man than God. This doesn't mean I don't believe He *is* God, but that's just how I imagine Him.

2. It may help to have the group consider some of the things Jesus said to people as recorded in the Gospels. Here are a few to get you started:

Matthew 23:13–33, including, 'Woe to you, teachers of the law and Pharisees, you hypocrites! You travel over land and sea to win a single convert, and when you have succeeded, you make them twice as much a child of hell as you are' (v15).

Luke 9:59–62, including, 'Let the dead bury their own dead, but you go and proclaim the kingdom of God' (v60).

John 6:51–58, including, 'Very truly I tell you, the truth, unless you eat the flesh of the Son of Man and drink his blood, you have no life in you' (v53).

3. It may help to recall some of the reasons you came up with in the previous session when considering why people choose not to believe in God.

4. In both these verses the speaker claims to be, 'the Alpha and the Omega', yet in the first instance the speaker is identified as 'the Lord God', while the second speaker identifies Himself as Jesus in verse 16.

5. This will be considered more fully in session 6 when we look at what we believe about salvation. However, it is worth spending a little time on this now, as our salvation is dependent on the fact that Jesus is God. If He wasn't, His sacrifice would not have been sufficient to pay for our sins!

6. This is the question about belief shaping how we live, and it's not an easy one! Again it is worth thinking of one or two practical examples from your own life to share with the group to help get the discussion going.

7. If you decide to run this Discussion Starter as a role-playing exercise, it is worth knowing that the Jehovah's Witnesses believe that Jesus is a spiritual being, God's first creation, but certainly not God.

People may find the Jehovah's Witness role hard to play, in which case feel free to substitute this with another role of your choosing.

Week 3: I Believe Jesus is Human

Following on from the previous session, this one focuses on the fact that Jesus is human, and during His time on earth He was subjected to a fallen body just like ours.

Opening Icebreaker

The aim of this exercise is to get the group to think about what makes us human. The reasons do not have to be confined to things which are exclusively human, and may

include anything in the following areas:
- parts of the body, such as hands, eyes and hearts
- physical feelings, such as hunger and pain
- emotional feelings, such as joy, envy and compassion
- actions, such as speaking and walking.

Discussion Starters

1. Again, this will be considered more fully in session 6: 'I Believe in Salvation'. However, it is worth spending a little time to consider the need for Jesus to be a human in order to save us, since only a human could pay the price owed to God by all humanity.

2. Here are some of the verses that list Jesus' human attributes:
- Physical body: Matthew 7:28, 15:30, 17:2, 26:7 and 27:34. Mark 8:23, 9:36 and 15:39. Luke 2:6–7, 2:40 and 8:46. John 19:33–34.
- Physical feelings: Matthew 4:2, 8:24, 9:10 and 13:1. John 4:6, 19:28, 30.
- Emotional feelings: Matthew 8:10, 9:36 and 26:37. Mark 3:5. Luke 10:21 and 22:44.
- Human actions: Matthew 4:12, 18, 8:3, 13:34 and 20:34. Mark 5:32 and 15:19. Luke 22:44. John 11:35.

3. This is the question about belief shaping how we live. As before, it is worth thinking of a couple of practical examples from your own life to share with the group to help get the discussion going. For me, knowing that Jesus has also experienced suffering as a human shapes how I deal with suffering. It doesn't remove the suffering, but it gives me comfort and encouragement at such times.

4. These were popular beliefs during the first few centuries of the Church's existence. In their belief that Jesus is God, such teachings sought to remove Him from any suffering, which means Jesus could not have really

experienced what it is like to live as a human in this fallen world.

5. Even though Jesus now has a perfect, new body, He is still a human. This Discussion Starter is more about this fact than that He rules over all things – though that's an awesome fact in itself! The aim is to see just how committed God is to humanity, so much so that He is now eternally human Himself.

It is also worth considering our response to this in terms of loving others and sharing the Gospel.

6. I say that 'Lord' is not a common title, but this is not entirely true in the UK, where we still have Peers of the Realm. However, we no longer use this title in the sense of paying obeisance to someone or serving them. When we talk about Jesus as 'Lord' we use it in this older, reverential sense, and it is this that should be lived out in our lives.

It is worth having an example from your own life to get the discussion started.

7. Again, it may be worth role-playing this scenario with members of the group taking turns at being the believer or the non-believer.

Week 4: I Believe in the Holy Spirit

This session focuses on the person and godhood of the Holy Spirit together with His role in the lives of believers.

Opening Icebreaker

Here are some concept words you could use when playing this game: acceleration, anger, anti-gravity, boredom, deceit, discovery, fragrance, greed, happiness, homesickness, hunger, indecision, melancholy, revolution, scepticism, shock, strength, surprise, tidiness, weight-loss.

The point of this group exercise, as far as the topic is concerned, is that because people tend to think of the Holy Spirit more as a concept than as a person (God), it makes it harder to relate to Him.

Discussion Starters

1. This is the same question I asked the group of teenagers and since this is mentioned in the Opening Our Eyes section, it may be worth asking the group what they would have answered before reading this. Getting people to close their eyes may help, and you might even ask them what image comes to mind when they hear the phrases, 'God the Father' and 'Jesus Christ'.

2. As mentioned, these pictures tell us about the Holy Spirit rather than describe His appearance or form. Some things to consider include the unpredictable nature of wind, the life-sustaining effect of water and the purifying qualities of fire, but this is by no means an exhaustive list.

3. This relates to the previous Discussion Starter about the pictures of the Holy Spirit. Consider the impersonal nature of these elements and the fact they are all somewhat ethereal and unholdable (which isn't a word, but you get the idea).

4. Although being filled with the Holy Spirit is not mentioned in the Creed, I have included this Discussion Starter as it is an important aspect of the Holy Spirit's work in the lives of God's people. It also tends to bring

out some lively debate, so it is worth making sure you do not spend too much time on this.

Here is my suggestion on what it means to be filled with the Holy Spirit, but feel free to disagree:
- We are filled with the fullness of His person – this is when the Holy Spirit comes to dwell in us when we first believe (see Eph. 1:13)
- We are filled with His power – which is sufficient for every occasion (see Eph. 3:16,20)
- We are filled with perfection – by which I mean the Holy Spirit is transforming us to become increasingly like Jesus (see 2 Cor. 3:18).

5. This is a much bigger task than it might at first appear, so here are just a few verses that describe some of the tasks the Holy Spirit performs. It may be worth preparing some specific ones beforehand.
- He moves people to share the good news (Acts 1:8)
- He confirms this message of good news through demonstrations of power (1 Cor. 2:4)
- He convicts hearers of their sin (1 Thess. 1:5)
- He moves hearers to put their faith in Christ (2 Cor. 4:13)
- He gives the believer new life in Christ (John 3:8)
- He cleanses us from our sin so we are holy before Him (1 Cor. 6:11)
- He comes to dwell in the new believer (2 Cor. 1:22)
- He gives us assurance that we are God's children (Rom. 8:16)
- He guides us into truth and give us understanding (John 16:13)
- He leads us in the way that God says is best to live (Gal. 5:16)
- He gives us the power to live that way (2 Tim. 1:7)
- He changes us to be more like Christ (2 Cor. 3:18)
- He speaks with us, teaching and reminding us (John 14:26)

- He gives us the words to say to defend our faith (Luke 12:11–12)
- He helps us to pray and prays on our behalf (Rom. 8:27)
- He has fellowship with us and loves us (Rom 5:5)
- He dwells among His people, giving gifts to build up the Church (1 Cor. 3:16; 12:7–11).

6. Here's the 'belief shapes action' question, and again it is worth being prepared with the difference your belief in the Holy Spirit makes to your daily life. It is worth being specific about exactly which beliefs shape which areas. For example, the belief that the Holy Spirit lives in you will shape your life differently to the belief that the Holy Spirit gives gifts to build up the Church.

7. As before, this could be a role-playing exercise. Enjoy playing the part of the teenager!

Week 5: I Believe in the Church

The focus of this session is the Church, specifically the universal, united community of the saints (believers) as opposed to individual denominations or local churches.

Opening Icebreaker

This group exercise is simply to make the point that the word 'church' in English doesn't always refer to the people of God, but can be legitimately used in other contexts.

The seven meanings of this word are:
- the universal people of God (the Church)
- local gatherings of Christians
- buildings where Christians meet (or used to meet)
- denominations, such as the Baptist Church or Roman Catholic Church

- a service (eg, 'I don't want to be late for church')
- Christian cults, such as the Church of Jesus Christ of Latter Day Saints
- knowledge and experience of Christianity (eg, 'reaching out to the un-churched').

Discussion Starters:

1. If people in the group have had experience of church splits, it would be worth discussing these. Also consider events like the Protestant Reformation, the separation of the Eastern Orthodox Church and Roman Catholic Church, and the formation of the Baptist and Methodist Churches.

2. As briefly explained in the Open Our Eyes section, the 'saints' are those God has declared holy. Take time to discuss what the group understands by the term 'holy' together with how people can be holy.

You may also want to talk, albeit for a short time, about people like Saint Augustine or Saint Christopher being 'saints', and how this conflicts with the biblical view.

3. It is worth reminding the group again, as we are now over half way through our studies on the Creed, that what we believe shapes how we live. In light of this, it would be good to challenge the group that if they really believe what they claim to believe about the Church it will make a significant difference to their daily lives.

Consider for example the belief that the Church is 'one'. If we really believe this, we will strive for this unity in our local church and live it out in our interaction with Christians outside our specific denomination.

4. While it is fine to discuss marriage in the light of what it may teach about Christ and the Church, try to avoid letting the group get drawn into a discussion about the roles of husbands and wives as it can be a contentious topic for

some and this is not the purpose of the Discussion Starter.

5. I did not tackle the term 'apostolic' in the Opening Our Eyes section, though it is mentioned in Belief in Action. It is not a reference to 'apostolic succession', which is the Roman Catholic teaching that the popes can be traced all the way back to the apostle Peter. Instead it is a reference to the fact that the Church was built on the teachings of the apostles (see Acts 2:42 and 1 Cor. 3:10–11). To be 'apostolic' is to be built on the solid foundation of Scriptural truth, such as that covered in the Creed.

6. This is more than asking people to list their victories over temptation in their quest to live a pure life. By 'holy' I am referring to the call for God's people to be different in their thoughts, speech and actions to those who do not know God. It may be worth clarifying this by asking the group how their lives have been shaped by biblical, rather than worldly, values.

7. There are those who believe that their particular denomination is the true Church, to the exclusion of all others – the Roman Catholic Church, for example – so even if you do not know anyone from such a denomination, it should still be possible to role-play this scenario.

The key points to get across here are the unity of the Church as a whole, what makes someone part of the Church and what does not.

Week 6: I Believe in Salvation

This session focuses on salvation in the context of the forgiveness of sins and our access to God – all that was done for us through Jesus' death on the cross.

Opening Icebreaker

The point of this group exercise is to help draw out the five points of salvation that are covered in the Opening Our Eyes section. That said, it's a great little card game – have fun!

The rules are simple: each player is dealt five cards, with the remaining cards being placed face down in a stack. The aim is for each player to save up sets of four cards (four 3s, four aces, etc), which players place in front of themselves.

The players take turns to ask any opponent if they have a particular rank of cards, for example, 'Elisha, do you have any Jacks?' The asking player must already have at least one card of the requested rank in their possession.

If the opponent has any of the requested cards, they must be given to the asking player, who then gets another go. If the opponent does not have the requested card, they must say 'go fish' and the asking player picks up a card from the stack. Their turn is over and it becomes the turn of the player who said 'go fish'.

Any player who runs out of cards must pick up five from the stack of spare cards in the middle. Play continues until the stack is empty.

The winner is the player who saves up the most sets of four cards.

Discussion Starters:

1. The two most common explanations for us being condemned because of Adam are that as the first man he was a representative of all humankind, and that, as the father of the human race, all of us were, in a sense, 'in' him.

Whether or not this is fair is entirely a matter of opinion, but it may be worth considering whether it is fair that, through faith in Christ, some of us can be saved from that condemnation.

2. The reasons for God being cut off from the Israelites, despite His proximity to them, are really the same as the reasons why God and man were separated at the Fall. However, it is worth taking the time to consider the role the Law played in that relationship.

3. While these verses give the easy answer, 'those who believe', it is worth considering exactly what we mean by believe. After all, people who believe God exists are not necessarily saved. What is it that we have to believe in order to be saved? And what about James' insistence that true faith is accompanied by actions? (see James 2:14–20)

4. This overlaps somewhat with Discussion Starter 2, since the reasons God was still cut off from the Israelites were the very reasons Jesus came to save us. However, it is worth considering some of the discussions from sessions two and three concerning why Jesus had to be both human and God in order to save us.

5. These two verses talk about God forgiving our sins. Other verses that might also help with this discussion are Isaiah 38:17 and 43:25. This is a somewhat subjective Discussion Starter, so it may be worth spending some time in silence as the group consider the comprehensive nature of this forgiveness in their own lives before sharing their feeling on the matter.

6. This is the 'belief in action'. The key areas to focus on in this Discussion Starter are:
• How we see ourselves in the light of God's forgiveness – do we beat ourselves up and wallow in guilt?

- How we treat others – do we refuse to forgive people who sin against us?
- How we honour God – do we live in a way that demonstrates our gratitude or do we take that forgiveness for granted?

Some may find it difficult to share such personal information, so it is worth being prepared to share examples from your life first to encourage others to participate.

7. This is a great exercise to role-play, as it will force people to consider how to share the gospel with someone who has no prior knowledge of Christianity. Stress the need to use as little Christian jargon as possible.

Week 7: I Believe in Eternal Life

Building on the previous session, this one looks at the promise of new bodies and everlasting life with God in the new heaven and earth – everything that has been assured for us through Jesus' resurrection.

Opening Icebreaker

This is a fairly straightforward group exercise, though it may be worth having some examples ready from your own life to get the Icebreaker going.

The point is to see that our hopes, wishes, dreams and plans for the future affect how we live today. The same should, of course, be true of our hope for eternal life.

Discussion Starters

1. If everyone in the group is already in agreement that life after death involves living forever with God in the new heavens and the new earth, it may be worth asking them what non-Christians think the Bible teaches about 'going to heaven'.

Try to avoid allowing the group to spend a long time discussing end-times interpretations, such as the Millennium and the Rapture.

2. I have included this Discussion Starter as it was something that used to trouble me as a young believer (and sometimes still does), mainly when going through difficulties or struggling with issues such as temptation.

Three reasons that seem to make sense in response are that:
- God uses the events of our lives to teach us dependence on Him and to change us to be more like Jesus
- we have a message of good news to share with the world around us and need to be here to do so
- the Bible encourages us to store up treasure in heaven – eternal rewards that depend on how we live our lives.

If these things are true, and we really believe them, our lives will be very different to those of people who do not know God!

3. Talking about our lives being different because of what we believe, here is the 'belief shapes life' question. These two passages both speak about the new heavens and new earth, the perfect world that has been promised to us by God.

It is worth considering the answers from the previous Discussion Starter (or the three points I have suggested above).

As usual, it may be helpful to share examples of how your belief in life after death has shaped your own life, to get the ball rolling.

4. This is a 'belief shapes life' question with a difference as you will be considering something you hopefully do not believe! As you tackle this Discussion Starter, it is worth getting the group to think about why they would live in the ways they suggest.

5. Although I touched on this briefly in the notes for Discussion Starter 2, it would be good to devote some time to the doctrine of rewards as people tend to be somewhat polarised on this topic.

It may be worth considering the following verses to help with this discussion: Isaiah 40:10, Matthew 6:1ff, Colossians 3:23–24, 1 Timothy 6:17–19, Hebrews 11:6, 24–26 and Revelation 22:12.

6. and 7. These final two Discussion Starters could both be used as role-playing exercises. If any in the group are uncomfortable playing the part of a humanist, or are uncertain what humanists believe, you could substitute these with people who don't believe in resurrection and believe there is no life after death.

Cover to Cover Every Day
Gain deeper knowledge of the Bible

Each issue of these bimonthly daily Bible-reading notes gives you insightful commentary on a book of the Old and New Testaments with reflections on a psalm each weekend by Philip Greenslade.

Enjoy contributions from two well-known authors every two months and over a five-year period you will be taken through the entire Bible.

Only £2.99 each (plus p&p)
£15.95 for UK annual subscription (bimonthly, p&p included)
£14.25 for annual email subscription
(available from www.cwr.org.uk/store)

 Individual issues available in epub/Kindle formats

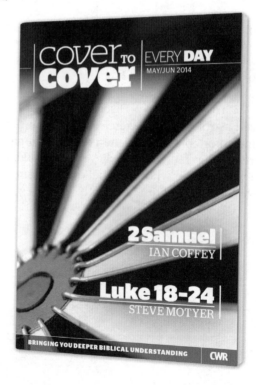

Prices correct at time of printing
To order visit www.cwr.org.uk/subscriptions
Available online or from Christian bookshops.

Cover to Cover Complete – NIV Edition
Read through the Bible chronologically

Take an exciting, year-long journey through the Bible, following events as they happened.

- See God's strategic plan of redemption unfold across the centuries
- Increase your confidence in the Bible as God's inspired message
- Come to know your heavenly Father in a deeper way.

The full text of the NIV provides an exhilarating reading experience and is augmented by our beautiful:

- Illustrations
- Maps
- Charts
- Diagrams
- Timeline

Key Scripture verses and devotional thoughts make each day's reading more meaningful.

ISBN: 978-1-85345-804-0

Dramatic new resource

1 Peter – Good reasons for hope
by Dave Edwins

As Christians, what reason do we have to hope in a hostile world? How can we respond to unjust suffering? Peter's letter to his fellow Christians shows that then, as now, the answer lies in who we are in Christ.

72-page booklet, 210x148mm
ISBN: 978-1-78259-088-0

The bestselling *Cover to Cover* Bible Study Series

1 Corinthians
Growing a Spirit-filled church
ISBN: 978-1-85345-374-8

2 Corinthians
Restoring harmony
ISBN: 978-1-85345-551-3

1 Peter
Good reasons for hope
ISBN: 978-1-78259-088-0

1 Timothy
*Healthy churches –
effective Christians*
ISBN: 978-1-85345-291-8

23rd Psalm
The Lord is my shepherd
ISBN: 978-1-85345-449-3

2 Timothy and Titus
Vital Christianity
ISBN: 978-1-85345-338-0

Acts 1–12
Church on the move
ISBN: 978-1-85345-574-2

Acts 13–28
To the ends of the earth
ISBN: 978-1-85345-592-6

Barnabas
Son of encouragement
ISBN: 978-1-85345-911-5

Bible Genres
Hearing what the Bible really says
ISBN: 978-1-85345-987-0

Daniel
Living boldly for God
ISBN: 978-1-85345-986-3

Ecclesiastes
*Hard questions and
spiritual answers*
ISBN: 978-1-85345-371-7

Elijah
A man and his God
ISBN: 978-1-85345-575-9

Ephesians
Claiming your inheritance
ISBN: 978-1-85345-229-1

Esther
For such a time as this
ISBN: 978-1-85345-511-7

Fruit of the Spirit
Growing more like Jesus
ISBN: 978-1-85345-375-5

Galatians
Freedom in Christ
ISBN: 978-1-85345-648-0

Genesis 1–11
Foundations of reality
ISBN: 978-1-85345-404-2

God's Rescue Plan
*Finding God's fingerprints
on human history*
ISBN: 978-1-85345-294-9

Great Prayers of the Bible
Applying them to our lives today
ISBN: 978-1-85345-253-6

Hebrews
Jesus – simply the best
ISBN: 978-1-85345-337-3

Hosea
The love that never fails
ISBN: 978-1-85345-290-1

Isaiah 1–39
Prophet to the nations
ISBN: 978-1-85345-510-0

Isaiah 40–66
Prophet of restoration
ISBN: 978-1-85345-550-6

James
Faith in action
ISBN: 978-1-85345-293-2

Jeremiah
The passionate prophet
ISBN: 978-1-85345-372-4

John's Gospel
Exploring the seven miraculous signs
ISBN: 978-1-85345-295-6

Joseph
The power of forgiveness and reconciliation
ISBN: 978-1-85345-252-9

Judges 1-8
The spiral of faith
ISBN: 978-1-85345-681-7

Judges 9-21
Learning to live God's way
ISBN: 978-1-85345-910-8

Mark
Life as it is meant to be lived
ISBN: 978-1-85345-233-8

Moses
Face to face with God
ISBN: 978-1-85345-336-6

Names of God
Exploring the depths of God's character
ISBN: 978-1-85345-680-0

Nehemiah
Principles for life
ISBN: 978-1-85345-335-9

Parables
Communicating God on earth
ISBN: 978-1-85345-340-3

Philemon
From slavery to freedom
ISBN: 978-1-85345-453-0

Philippians
Living for the sake of the gospel
ISBN: 978-1-85345-421-9

Prayers of Jesus
Hearing His heartbeat
ISBN: 978-1-85345-647-3

Proverbs
Living a life of wisdom
ISBN: 978-1-85345-373-1

Revelation 1-3
Christ's call to the Church
ISBN: 978-1-85345-461-5

Revelation 4-22
The Lamb wins! Christ's final victory
ISBN: 978-1-85345-411-0

Rivers of Justice
Responding to God's call to righteousness today
ISBN: 978-1-85345-339-7

Ruth
Loving kindness in action
ISBN: 978-1-85345-231-4

The Covenants
God's promises and their relevance today
ISBN: 978-1-85345-255-0

The Creed
Belief in action
ISBN: 978-1-78259-202-0

The Divine Blueprint
God's extraordinary power in ordinary lives
ISBN: 978-1-85345-292-5

The Holy Spirit
Understanding and experiencing Him
ISBN: 978-1-85345-254-3

The Image of God
His attributes and character
ISBN: 978-1-85345-228-4

The Kingdom
Studies from Matthew's Gospel
ISBN: 978-1-85345-251-2

The Letter to the Colossians
In Christ alone
ISBN: 978-1-85345-405-9

The Letter to the Romans
Good news for everyone
ISBN: 978-1-85345-250-5

The Lord's Prayer
Praying Jesus' way
ISBN: 978-1-85345-460-8

The Prodigal Son
Amazing grace
ISBN: 978-1-85345-412-7

The Second Coming
Living in the light of Jesus' return
ISBN: 978-1-85345-422-6

The Sermon on the Mount
Life within the new covenant
ISBN: 978-1-85345-370-0

The Tabernacle
Entering into God's presence
ISBN: 978-1-85345-230-7

The Ten Commandments
Living God's Way
ISBN: 978-1-85345-593-3

The Uniqueness of our Faith
What makes Christianity distinctive?
ISBN: 978-1-85345-232-1

For current prices or to order visit www.cwr.org.uk/store
Available online or from Christian bookshops.

SMALL GROUP
ToolBox

Exploring vital issues of Christian growth and discipleship

'This exciting series of small group resources offers essential study material in very accessible formats, each covering four weeks.'

Discovering Your Spiritual Gifts
ISBN: 978-1-85345-765-4

Guidance
ISBN: 978-1-78259-053-8

Hearing God
ISBN: 978-1-85345-764-7

Strong Faith in Tough Times
ISBN: 978-1-78259-054-5

Also available from April 2014:

Building Character Through Tough Times
ISBN: 978-1-78259-234-1

Identity
ISBN: 978-1-78259-235-8

For current prices and to order visit www.cwr.org.uk/toolbox.
Available online or from Christian bookshops.

Courses and seminars

Publishing and media

Conference facilities

Transforming lives

CWR's vision is to enable people to experience personal transformation through applying God's Word to their lives and relationships.

Our Bible-based training and resources help people around the world to:

- Grow in their walk with God
- Understand and apply Scripture to their lives
- Resource themselves and their church
- Develop pastoral care and counselling skills
- Train for leadership
- Strengthen relationships, marriage and family life and much more.

Our insightful writers provide daily Bible-reading notes and other resources for all ages, and our experienced course designers and presenters have gained an international reputation for excellence and effectiveness.

CWR's Training and Conference Centres in Surrey and East Sussex, England, provide excellent facilities in idyllic settings – ideal for both learning and spiritual refreshment.

CWR Applying God's Word
to everyday life and relationships

CWR, Waverley Abbey House,
Waverley Lane, Farnham,
Surrey GU9 8EP, UK

Telephone: **+44 (0)1252 784700**
Email: **info@cwr.org.uk**
Website: **www.cwr.org.uk**

Registered Charity No 294387
Company Registration No 1990308

NATIONAL DISTRIBUTORS

UK: (and countries not listed below)
CWR, Waverley Abbey House, Waverley Lane, Farnham, Surrey GU9 8EP.
Tel: (01252) 784700 Outside UK (44) 1252 784700

AUSTRALIA: KI Entertainment, Unit 21 317-321 Woodpark Road, Smithfield, New South Wales 2164. Tel: 1 800 850 777 Fax: 02 9604 3699. Email: sales@kientertainment.com.au

CANADA: David C Cook Distribution Canada, PO Box 98, 55 Woodslee Avenue, Paris, Ontario N3L 3E5. Tel: 1800 263 2664 Email: joy.kearley@davidccook.ca

GHANA: Challenge Enterprises of Ghana, PO Box 5723, Accra.
Tel: (021) 222437/223249 Fax: (021) 226227 Email: ceg@africaonline.com.gh

HONG KONG: Cross Communications Ltd, 1/F, 562A Nathan Road, Kowloon.
Tel: 2780 1188 Fax: 2770 6229 Email: cross@crosshk.com

INDIA: Crystal Communications, Plot No. 125, Road No. 7, T.M.C, Mahendra Hills, East Marredpally, Secunderabad - 500026 Tel/Fax: (040) 27737145
Email: crystal_edwj@rediffmail.com

KENYA: Keswick Books and Gifts Ltd, PO Box 10242-00400, Nairobi.
Tel: (020) 2226047/312639 Email: sales.keswick@africaonline.co.ke

MALAYSIA: Canaanland Distributors Sdn Bhd, No. 25 Jalan PJU 1A/41B, NZX Commercial Centre, Ara Jaya, 47301 Petaling Jaya, Selangor. Tel: (03) 7885 0540/1/2 Fax: (03) 7885 0545 Email: info@canaanland.com.my

Salvation Publishing & Distribution Sdn Bhd, 23 Jalan SS 2/64, 47300 Petaling Jaya, Selangor. Tel: (03) 78766411/78766797 Fax: (03) 78757066/78756360
Email: info@salvationbookcentre.com

NEW ZEALAND: KI Entertainment, Unit 21 317-321 Woodpark Road, Smithfield, New South Wales 2164, Australia. Tel: 0 800 850 777 Fax: +612 9604 3699
Email: sales@kientertainment.com.au

NIGERIA: FBFM, Helen Baugh House, 96 St Finbarr's College Road, Akoka, Lagos. Tel: (+234) 01-7747429, 08075201777, 08186337699, 08154453905
Email: fbfm_1@yahoo.com

PHILIPPINES: OMF Literature Inc, 776 Boni Avenue, Mandaluyong City.
Tel: (02) 531 2183 Fax: (02) 531 1960 Email: gloadlaon@omflit.com

SINGAPORE: Alby Commercial Enterprises Pte Ltd, 95 Kallang Avenue #04-00, AIS Industrial Building, 339420. Tel: (65) 629 27238 Fax: (65) 629 27235
Email: marketing@alby.com.sg

SOUTH AFRICA: Life Media & Distribution, Unit 20, Tungesten Industrial Park, 7 C R Swart Drive, Strydompark 2125 Tel: (+27) 0117924277 Fax: (+27) 0117924512 Email: orders@lifemedia.co.za

SRI LANKA: Christombu Publications (Pvt) Ltd, Bartleet House, 65 Braybrooke Place, Colombo 2. Tel: (+941) 2421073/2447665. Email: christombupublications@gmail.com

USA: David C Cook Distribution Canada, PO Box 98, 55 Woodslee Avenue, Paris, Ontario N3L 3E5, Canada. Tel: 1800 263 2664. Email: joy.kearley@davidccook.ca

For email addresses, visit the CWR website: www.cwr.org.uk
CWR is a Registered Charity - Number 294387
CWR is a Limited Company registered in England - Registration Number 1990308